BEAUTY HACKS

NAIL, HAND, AND FEET HACKS

YOUR NAIL NUISANCES SOLVED!

BY MARY BOONE

CAPSTONE PRESS
a capstone imprint

Savvy Books are published by Capstone Press,
1710 Roe Crest Drive, North Mankato, Minnesota 56003
www.mycapstone.com

Library of Congress Cataloging-in-Publication Data
Library of Congress Cataloging-in-Publication data is
available on the Library of Congress website.
ISBN 978-1-5157-6830-2 (library binding)
ISBN 978-1-5157-6834-0 (eBook PDF)

Editorial Credits
Mandy Robbins, editor; Aruna Rangarajan, designer;
Kelli Lageson and Morgan Walters, media researchers;
Kathy McColley, production specialist

Image Credits
All photos by Capstone Studio: Karon Dubke, except:
Capstone Press: Aruna Rangarajan, 5; Ella Banken: 48, inset;
iStockphoto: nycshooter, cover; Shutterstock: Africa Studio, 11 (milk
and tea), 23 (bottom), 43, aimy27feb, cover (back cover top right), 38
(bottom), Ann Haritonenko, 4, 20 (right), 27 (top), Antonio Guillem,
14, Ariwasabi, 16 (bottom), Artmim, cover (back cover bottom left),
bigacis, 9, 11 (Greek yogurt and oatmeal), Billion Photos, 8 (top),
bjphotographs, 11 (beef), Bogachyova Arina, 11 (avocado), boivin
nicolas, 22, Boonchuay1970, 11 (seaweed), D7INAMI7S, 11 (coconut),
Davydenko Yuliia, 11 (oysters), Day2505, 32, top, Dean Drobot,
44 (bottom), Dmitry A, 40, domnitsky, 11 (rosemary), DONOT6_
STUDIO, 8 (middle), Dragon Images, 23 (top), 26 (bottom), Dzha33,
35, file404, 21 (right), fotyma, cover (back cover top right), Gino
Santa Maria, 47 (bottom), Halfpoint, 45 (top), Ivan Marjanovic, 20
(left), jonny89, 27 (bottom right), Kaponia Aliaksei, 6, Kayo, 7 (top),
KhunChaiSpy, 11 (kiwi), Lazuin, 19, matin, 11 (quinoa), musicphone,
2, 24, 48, NANOM, 11 (bell peppers), Natalia Klenova, 10 (bottom),
Olena Yakobchuk, 34, Origination Nes, 38 (top), photka, 33 (plastic
bag), Pun foto gallery, 11 (pumpkin seeds), Raisman, 45 (bottom),
ratmaner, 16 (top), Rawpixel.com, 21 (left), Richard Griffin, 11
(lobster), Safargalieva Ilsiar, 11 (walnuts), Sergey Tay, 27 (left),
31 (middle), sirtravelalot, 12, SOMMAI, 11 (lentils), SunCity, 42
(background), Svitlana Sokolova, 46, Thanthip Homs, 11 (spinach),
topnatthapon, 7 (bottom), Valua Vitaly, 36 (top right), Vicki Vale,
7 (middle), violetblue, 8 (bottom), warat42, 11 (collard greens),
WAYHOME studio, 17, xpixel, 11 (chocolate)
Design elements: Shutterstock

Printed and bound in the USA.
010373F17

TABLE OF CONTENTS

Your hands and feet are important body parts. Without them, you'd have a hard time walking, dancing, playing an instrument, or even picking up a pencil. But are you giving them the love and attention they deserve?

GIVE YOUR LIMBS A LITTLE LOVE

NAIL CARE ESSENTIALS

Taking care of your hands, feet, and nails is as important as washing your face or brushing your teeth. Cracked heels, ragged nails, and sweaty palms can hurt your confidence. Itchy, smelly feet or discolored nails can be embarrassing. But there's more to it than that. Caring for your hands, feet, and nails can actually have long-lasting health benefits. Without regular care, your hands and feet run the risk of picking up an infection.

You can make your hands, feet, and nails a priority. The projects in this book will help. All you need are a few handy tools and products.

SUPPLIES NEEDED

* aluminum foil
* antibacterial soap
* colored nail polish
* cotton balls, squares, and swabs
* cotton gloves
* felt squares
* four-way nail buffer
* gentle lotion
* glass nail file
* 91-percent isopropyl alcohol
* orangewood sticks (used to push back cuticles or clean fingernails)
* nail clippers
* nail glue
* nail polish base coat
* nail polish top coat
* nail polish remover
* pumice stone
* toe separators
* tweezers

"I don't like plain nails. I get sad."

–Zooey Deschanel

Your diet can play a big role in the look of your skin and nails. Eating the right foods can help your skin and nails stay healthy, strong, and free of infection. Stock your kitchen with these super foods for glowing skin and strong nails.

CHAPTER 1

FOODS FOR HEALTHY NAILS AND SKIN

BERRY GOOD NEWS

Blueberries are loaded with antioxidants, vitamins, and minerals. They've been proven to help slow or reverse damage caused by the sun, pollution, and stress. They can also boost your body's immune system, so you'll be less likely to develop skin infections.

EGGS MAKE NAILS STRONG

The protein in eggs is easier to digest than meat protein. And protein is a must for strong fingernails. Eggs are also a terrific source of the chemical biotin. Biotin can increase nail thickness and reduce splitting.

SUPERB SALMON

Do you struggle with brittle nails? Try eating more salmon. This fish is rich in B12, vitamin D, zinc, and protein. Each of these ingredients fuels nail growth.

Have you ever noticed that your nails are dark or off-color? If you don't get enough zinc in your diet, your nails may split or become discolored. Wild salmon provides more zinc than farm-raised salmon, so choose the wild option if you can.

NO SWEAT

Do you struggle with sweaty palms or feet? Grab a glass of tomato juice! Tomatoes shrink pores and reduce sweating. Drink one large glass of tomato juice daily for a week to see the difference. Keep up the daily habit, or switch to every other day to keep sweat at bay.

MILK BATH

Dry hands and feet can benefit from a soak in warm milk. The fat in milk moisturizes skin. Milk also has lactic acid in it. This chemical helps dead skin fall off. Pour three cups of whole milk into a microwave-safe bowl and heat until warm — not hot. Soak your hands in the milk for 15 minutes before rinsing with warm water. You can use this same method to soak your feet. Just pour the big bowl into a large, shallow pan. Soak 15 minutes, then rinse.

SWEET POTATO PERK

Sweet potatoes are packed with beta-carotene. Your body converts beta-carotene to vitamin A. Studies show that vitamin A can strengthen brittle nails, making them less likely to break or split.

MAYONNAISE

Mayonnaise is rich in eggs and oils, which means it can work wonders for hangnails and dry cuticles. Try treating your dry, cracked cuticles using one of these methods:

1. Put a scoop of mayonnaise in a small bowl and sink your fingertips into it. Soak for 10 minutes. Then rinse with warm water.

2. Try a whole-hand spa experience by slathering two spoonfuls of mayonnaise onto your palms. Rub the mayonnaise into your hands like it's lotion. Then put on a pair of cotton gloves. Leave the gloves on for at least one hour. Rinse well.

3. Slather your feet in mayo to soften dry rough skin. Wait two minutes, and then wipe off with a warm, wet cloth.

COCONUT OR OLIVE OIL

Dry feet can be uncomfortable or even painful. The good news is you can find relief as close as your kitchen cabinet. Coconut and olive oils both contain fatty acids that can help moisturize skin. Apply either type of oil to your feet. Then put on cotton socks. Leave the socks on overnight. Rinse your feet with warm, soapy water in the morning. Repeat several times a week until skin is soft and cracks are healed.

BAKING SODA SCRUB

Baking soda works magic on yellowing nails. Mix equal parts water and baking soda into a paste. Let it sit on your bare nails for 10 minutes. Scrub with an old toothbrush. Rinse with warm water, and go from drab to bright.

olive oil

coconut oil

baking soda

SUPER FOODS MAKE FOR SUPER SKIN AND NAILS

What you put in your body is as important as what you put on it — maybe even more important. The right vitamins and nutrients can go a long way toward keeping skin soft and nails strong. Hair and nails are made of the same chemical called keratin. Protein and iron are essential to keratin production. Certain meats and leafy greens have both. Antioxidants found in many fruits and vegetables protect against damage to all your cells, including your hair and nails. Magnesium, zinc, vitamin D, and other nutrients also boost hair and nail health.

SUPER FOOD BINGO

Make healthy eating fun by turning it into a game. Try to eat a Bingo row of these super foods each week.

avocados	lentils	kiwis	milk
collard greens	dark chocolate	grass-fed beef	coconut
green tea	bell peppers	rosemary	lobster
oatmeal	pumpkin seeds	spinach	Greek yogurt
seaweed	quinoa	walnuts	oysters

Before you start on manicures or nail art, healthy nails are a must. Give your hands some extra love. Use these tips for cleaning, trimming, and shaping your nails.

CHAPTER 2

NAIL CARE
BASICS

GET CLUED IN ON CLIPPERS

Nail clippers come in many styles and sizes. Nickel-plated clippers don't cost much, but they can dull quickly. That means you may have jagged results. You could spend a little more money for quality stainless-steel clippers that stay sharp longer. Be sure to have separate clippers for your toenails and fingernails. You don't want to spread bacteria or fungus from your feet to your hands or vice versa. It could lead to infections.

FIX A CRACKED NAIL

A torn or cracked nail doesn't have to be a disaster. To fix a tear, start with clean nails with no polish or base coat. Cut a piece of tea bag a little larger than the length and width of the crack. It will be a bandage for your broken nail.

Step 1: Use an orangewood stick to apply a drop of nail glue to the area around the tear.

Step 2: Use tweezers to place the tea bag over the break.

Step 3: When the glue is dry, use a buffer or file to smooth the tea bag and glue to match the surface of your nail. Then polish!

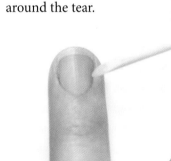

baking
soda

lemon
juice

BRIGHTENING SOAK

Dark nail polishes can stain nails or turn them yellow. You can remove those stains with a simple at-home soak. Mix together 2 teaspoons of water and 2 teaspoons of baking soda. Add 1 teaspoon of freshly squeezed lemon juice. Mix until the solution starts bubbling. Soak your nails in the mixture for 10 minutes. Rinse the mixture of in warm water, rubbing with a wet wash cloth for added cleaning power.

SKIP CUTICLE TRIMMING

The cuticle is that thin slice of skin along the bottom of your nail bed. It protects you from infection. Lots of people trim their cuticles, but doctors say there's no good reason for that. If you want your nails to look longer, try this trick. First soak your nails in warm water for five to 10 minutes to soften your cuticles. Then push them back gently with an orangewood stick.

FINE-TUNE YOUR FILING TECHNIQUE

Filing doesn't just shape your nails. It also helps prevent breakage and jagged tips. To avoid splits, always file your nails when they are dry. First use a nail clipper to trim them. Then get out your file to fine-tune the shape. File in one direction only. Avoid using a back-and-forth sawing motion. This can actually weaken your nails. Hold the file flat across your nail tip while filing. Holding the file at an angle will thin the nails.

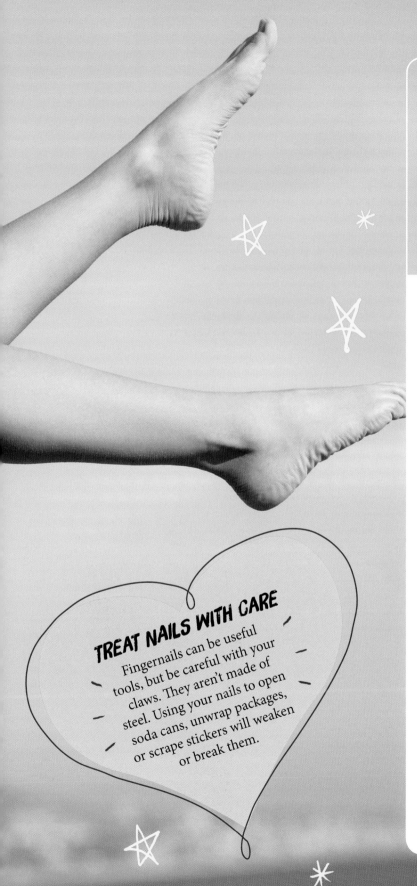

THE STRAIGHT TRUTH

Pressure from shoes can cause short toenails to curl down and grow into your skin. It's a painful condition called ingrown nails. Cutting the sides of your toenail at an angle can also cause ingrown nails. The short edges of your nails may curve into the skin as they grow out. Instead of rounding, trim your toenails straight across. And don't cut them too short. If you have an ingrown nail, the **American Academy of Dermatology** offers these tips:

✚ Soak your foot in warm salt water a few times a day. This will soften the skin around the ingrown nail and relieve pain. Dry your nails well after soaking.

✚ If there's room, stuff tiny pieces of clean cotton between the ingrown toenail and the skin for a little cushioning.

✚ Apply antibiotic cream to the sore spot to prevent an infection. Cover with a bandage for extra padding and protection.

✚ See a doctor if the pain continues or redness spreads from the ingrown nail.

TREAT NAILS WITH CARE

Fingernails can be useful tools, but be careful with your claws. They aren't made of steel. Using your nails to open soda cans, unwrap packages, or scrape stickers will weaken or break them.

KEEP TOOLS CLEAN

Small bits of fungus can live on metal surfaces for months. That's why it's important to clean your nail scissors and clippers every time you use them. To disinfect, fill a bowl with 91-percent isopropyl alcohol. Soak an old toothbrush in the alcohol for five minutes. Use the brush and a dab of antibacterial soap to scrub your clippers and scissors. Rinse them in hot water to kill germs. Follow up by soaking the nail tools in isopropyl alcohol for 30 minutes to kill any remaining bacteria or fungus. Dry with a towel. Store your tools in a clean place.

GLOVES
ARE YOUR FRIEND

Everyday life can take a toll on your fingernails. You can help protect them by wearing the right gloves. Rubber gloves can guard against damage from dishwashing or cleaning chemicals. If you're planting flowers or pulling weeds, wear gardening gloves. These can protect your nails from dirt and chemicals. Make sure the gloves fit well so you don't end up with blisters. It's also important to wear gloves in the winter. Cold weather tends to dry out nails and hands. Dry nails break more easily and are more likely to get infected.

PREVENT Hangnails

Hangnails are the dry, brittle bits of skin around your fingernails. They are caused by cold winter weather, nail biting, or spending a lot of time in water. It's tempting to tear off those hangnails, but don't! You will expose the living tissue underneath to bacteria and infection.

Here are some tips on how to treat a hangnail if you already have one:

1.
SOAK IT
Soften it by soaking your finger in warm water.

2.
CLIP IT
Clip the hangnail with cuticle scissors.

3.
TREAT IT
Apply antibacterial cream to prevent infection.

If you get hangnails often, try these tips:

▶ **QUIT BITING!** If you bite or pick at your nails, try to quit. Nail biting can cause hangnails and increases your chances of developing an infection.

▶ **MOISTURIZE!** Apply lotion to your hands and nail beds two to three times a day.

Find the Right FILE

Nail files come in a variety of materials including glass, ceramic, and padded cushion files. Professionals recommend avoiding metal files because they can damage nails.

A file's surface is known as its grit. It refers to the amount of abrasive grain particles that can fit into a square inch. When shopping for files, pay attention to the grit rating.

80 TO 100 GRIT: These coarse files are best for acrylic nails. These nails are the fake ones you would get put on at a salon.

600 TO 2400 GRIT: These ultra-fine files are used for buffing and shining all types of nails.

180 GRIT: These medium-grit files are good for shaping fingernail tips or toenails.

240 TO 600 GRIT: Fine-grit cushion files are gentle yet effective on natural nails. They can remove small bumps, ridges, or discoloration.

ROUND

Round nails are great for those who prefer short nails. They have straight sides but curve to follow the natural shape of the fingertip.

SQUARE

Square nails are flat on top with straight, sharp corners. This shape gives both short and long nails an edgy look.

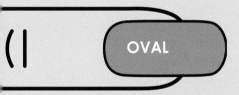

OVAL

Oval nails are filed down on the sides, so they tend to make fingers look slender.

SQUOVAL

This universally flattering shape features a straight top with softened corners.

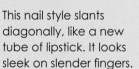

LIPSTICK

This nail style slants diagonally, like a new tube of lipstick. It looks sleek on slender fingers.

ALMOND

Nail walls are tapered to a round peak, like an almond. This shape works well with strong gel or acrylic nails.

STILETTO

This shape is like an almond, but with a sharper point and a wider base. Again, it works best on fake nails.

SHORT

Short nails work well for people who work with their hands a lot.

STOP BITING

1.

HYDRATION DISTRACTION
Carry a water bottle and take a sip of water when you're having a weak moment.

2.

POLISH PREVENTION
Paint your nails with clear or colored polish. You may be less likely to bite your nails if they look great.

3.

DE-STRESS
If you bite your nails because you're stressed, try yoga, meditation, or deep breathing to relax.

4.

BITTER BITER
If regular polish doesn't deter you, try nail-biting polish, which has a bitter taste. It is designed to discourage users from nibbling their nails.

If you bite your nails, you're not alone. Researchers say 6 percent of children and 45 percent of teenagers bite their nails. It can quickly become a habit and a serious problem. Regular nail biting can damage your teeth, nails, and the surrounding skin. Having ragged nails can also draw unwanted attention. To put an end to your nail biting, try one or more of these tricks and tips:

5.
BLOCK THE BITE
Put tape or bandages on the tips of your fingers so biting your nails isn't possible.

6.
KEEP YOUR TEETH BUSY
Chew gum or suck on mints throughout the day. Biting your nails will be tough if you have something else in your mouth.

7.
PUNISHMENT PREVENTION
Wear a rubber band or an elastic hairband around your wrist. Snap it whenever you get the urge to bite your nails.

8.
FRIENDLY INTERVENTION
Sometimes you bite your nails out of habit without even realizing it. Tell your friends to say something when they see you doing it.

CHAPTER 3

POLISH LIKE A PRO

Nail polish was first used in China as far back as 5,000 years ago. In ancient Egypt, your polish color told your class ranking. The lower class wore light colors. Royalty and high society women painted their nails red. Today you have the freedom to paint your nails however you like. Follow these tips to help make your manicures and pedicures look their best.

BASICS OF BASE COATS

Applying a base coat takes a little extra time, but it will make your manicure last longer. It also keeps dark nail polishes from staining your nails. Some base coats are made with ingredients to address different nail issues. For example, if the surface of your nails is uneven, choose a base coat designed to fill ridges. Read product labels to find one that fits your needs.

TOP IT OFF

After you've applied nail color, finish with a clear top coat. The top coat seals in the colored polish. When the polish is sealed, it does not chip as often. Top coats also give nails a shiny, glossy appearance. Don't use your base coat as a top coat or your top coat as a base. Base coats are usually thicker and stickier, which helps the nail polish stick. Top coats are thinner and are made to protect the polish from daily wear and tear.

WHICH POLISH

All polishes are not created equal. Use this polish primer to help you choose the right one for you.

GEL POLISH

Gels are brushed onto your nails in three steps — base coat, polish color, top coat. Each of these coats has to be hardened using a special ultra-violet light at a salon. Gel polish lasts up to three weeks. It must be properly removed to prevent damage to your nails.

GEL-LIKE POLISH

These polishes promise to deliver the shine and wear of a gel manicure without the use of UV lights. The good news for you is that means they're designed for use at home. These products last longer than traditional polishes and are cheaper than salon gel nails. But they don't last as long as light-cured gel nails.

SHOULD YOU USE?

NAIL WRAPS

Nail wraps can be applied like stickers and filed down to fit the shape of your nails. Nail wrappers can be a solid color, but more often they have wild, decorative, or interesting patterns. Using heat helps to minimize wrinkles or bumps in the wraps. A clear top coat helps the wraps last longer.

TRADITIONAL NAIL POLISH

Traditional manicures require a base coat, polish, and a top coat. These polishes are great for both at-home and salon manicures. The polish dries on its own, without any special equipment. A traditional polish manicure is less expensive than a gel manicure. However, it's also more prone to chipping and doesn't last as long.

DO-IT-YOURSELF MANICURE

Going to the spa is fun, but you can save some money by giving yourself an at-home manicure. Follow these steps for a beautiful basic manicure.

WHAT YOU NEED:

nail file + orangewood stick + cotton swabs + buffer

base coat + nail color + top coat + polish remover

WHAT TO DO:

Step 1: Start with clean, dry nails. Use a file to shape them however you want.

Step 2: Soak fingertips in warm water to soften cuticles. Gently push cuticles back with the slanted end of an orangewood stick. Dry nails.

Step 3: Wrap a bit of cotton around the pointed end of an orangewood stick, and dip the stick in warm water. Clean under nails, working from the center of each nail to the side. Dry nails.

Step 4: Use a buffer to give tips a smooth edge. Wash nails again to get off the filing grit, and dry completely.

Step 5: Apply the base coat using long strokes.

Step 6: When base coat is dry to the touch, apply polish with light strokes. Work from the base to the tip of the nail. Wait one to two minutes before applying a second coat. Two coats will give you more vibrant color.

Step 7: When polish is dry to the touch, apply a top coat. Brush the top coat underneath your nail tips for added protection.

Step 8: Use a cotton swab and nail polish remover to clean any excess polish from your cuticles or skin.

Make Neon Polish
POP

Neon polishes tend to go on thin and streaky. To make the color look smoother, apply a white or nude base coat first. Once that coat is dry to the touch, paint on two to three coats of neon polish. Finish with a top coat. This extra step will give more pop to your polish.

REVIVE GOOPY POLISH

Everybody has nail polish that's thick and goopy. Before you toss your favorite color, try to revive it! Use 91-percent isopropyl rubbing alcohol to do the trick. Add just a couple drops of alcohol into the polish, tighten the lid, and shake. If it's still too thick, add more alcohol, a drop at a time.

OMBRE NAILS CAN BE YOURS

WHAT YOU NEED:

base coat

two shades of nail polish in similar colors

top coat

triangle makeup sponges

polish remover

cotton swabs

WHAT YOU DO:

Step 1: Apply a base coat.

Step 2: When the base coat is dry, paint your nails with the lightest of the two colors. Allow the polish to dry completely.

Step 3: Choose a makeup sponge about the same width as your nail. Start by using the lighter color of polish to paint a horizontal line across the width of the sponge. Then paint a line of the darker polish under the first. Be sure the colors are painted right next to each other with no exposed sponge between the colors.

Step 4: Press the polished sponge on top of your nail. Make sure the colors will be stamped how you want them — either with the dark on the bottom or the light on the bottom. It's totally up to you. Lift and stamp again. Check after each stamp, and continue until you have the effect you want. Repeat steps 3 and 4 until all your nails are painted.

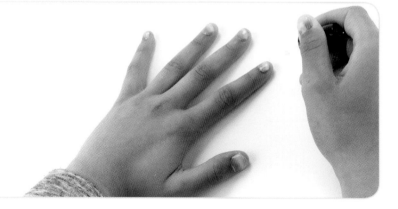

Step 5: Just before your nails are completely dry, add a top coat. Sponging can result in a bumpy surface. Adding a top coat before the bumps dry can help smooth them out. Several top coats may be needed to get a smooth, finished look.

Step 6: Use a cotton swap dipped in polish remover to clean any stray polish from your skin and cuticles.

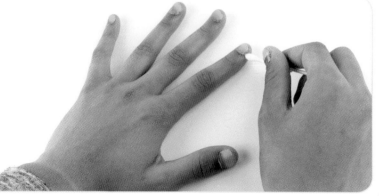

TIPS FOR FRENCH TIPS

A French manicure can be incredibly classy, with its pink or nude base and white nail tips. It can also be sassy if you opt for a color base and bold nail tips. Either way, the sharp line between colors is important. And best of all, it's easy to achieve using these steps.

WHAT YOU NEED:

base coat

+

base color (generally pink or nude, but any color can be used)

+

clear tape

+

cotton swabs

tip color (generally white, but any color will work)

+

polish remover

+

top coat

WHAT TO DO:

Step 1: Start with clean, dry nails that have been filed to your desired shape. The square or square-oval shape works best for French tips. Apply a clear base coat.

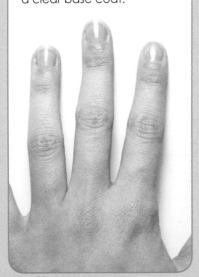

Step 2: Apply two coats of base color. Let polish dry fully between coats.

Step 3: Place a short piece of tape across each nail, right where your nail grows past the end of your fingertip.

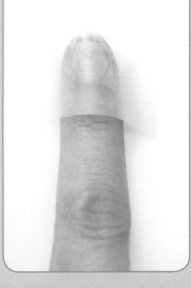

Step 4: Apply two coats of tip color above the tape line.

Step 5: When the tips are partially dry, remove the tape from each nail.

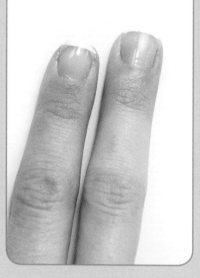

Step 6: Fix any smears with nail polish or a bit of polish remover on a cotton swab.

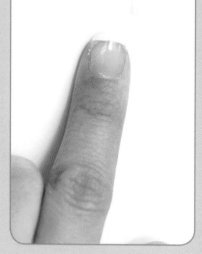

SPEED UP POLISH DRYING

The more rushed you are, the longer it seems to take polish to dry. Next time you're in a hurry, try one of these methods to speed up drying time.

Ice Water
Nail polish dries when it comes in contact with cool temperatures. Immediately after painting your nails, soak your fingertips in ice water for two to three minutes.

Freezer
While your nails are wet, stick your hands in the freezer for two minutes. Try to keep the door as closed as possible to save energy and to give your nails maximum cooling benefit.

Hairdryer
Use the cool setting on your dryer to speed up drying. Hold the dryer about a hand's length from your nails. Be sure not to smudge the nails of the hand holding the dryer.

Super Simple
NAIL ART

Nail art can be eye-catching but often looks difficult to do. It doesn't have to be. Try these easy nail art designs you can create with simple household items.

CLEAR TAPE

Paint a base coat, and let it dry for at least one hour. Apply strips of tape to your nails to create stripes, diagonal lines, or geometric shapes. Paint over the nail and tape with a different color polish. Pull the tape off while the polish is still wet for the crispest, cleanest lines. Let the polish dry completely, and add a clear top coat.

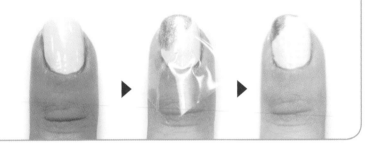

HOLE PUNCH REINFORCEMENT

These sticky circles can be used to create cool crescents at the base of your nails. Paint a base coat, and let it dry. Press the sticker firmly at the base of the nail to make crips lines. Apply two coats of colored polish. When the polish is dry, remove the stickers, and apply a clear top coat.

BOBBY PIN

Paint on a base color. When it's dry, use a straightened bobby pin to make dots. Just dip the plastic-coated end into a contrasting nail color and dot away. Let the dots dry fully before adding a clear top coat.

BEJEWEL YOUR FINGERS

Apply a base coat and two coats of nail polish as you would normally. Let polish dry completely. Next, apply a thick layer of top coat. While it's still wet, gently place rhinestones. Follow up with another layer of top coat over the rhinestones.

MAKE YOUR OWN NAIL STICKERS

Using nail decals or stickers is easier than painting patterns or pictures on your nails. You can buy nail stickers, but it's super easy to make your own.

large plastic
zip-top bag

several nail polish colors

base coat

scissors

tweezers

top coat

WHAT YOU DO:

Step 1: Tape the plastic bag to a flat surface. Make sure there are no folds or creases in the bag.

Step 2: Use nail polish to paint three or four 2-inch (5-centimeter) squares onto the plastic bag. Wait 10 minutes and paint a second coat.
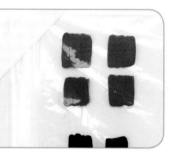

Step 3: Add any decoration you would like. Let polish squares dry overnight if possible.

Step 4: Peel dry polish off the plastic bag. Cut the squares into shapes such as lines, zig zags, tiny stars, or sunbursts.

Step 5: Apply a base coat and two coats of nail color. While the second coat is still sticky, use tweezers to carefully position the homemade stickers on your nails. When your nails are dry, finish with a clear top coat.
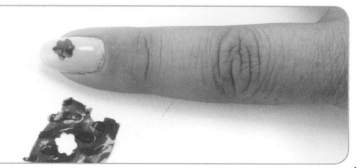

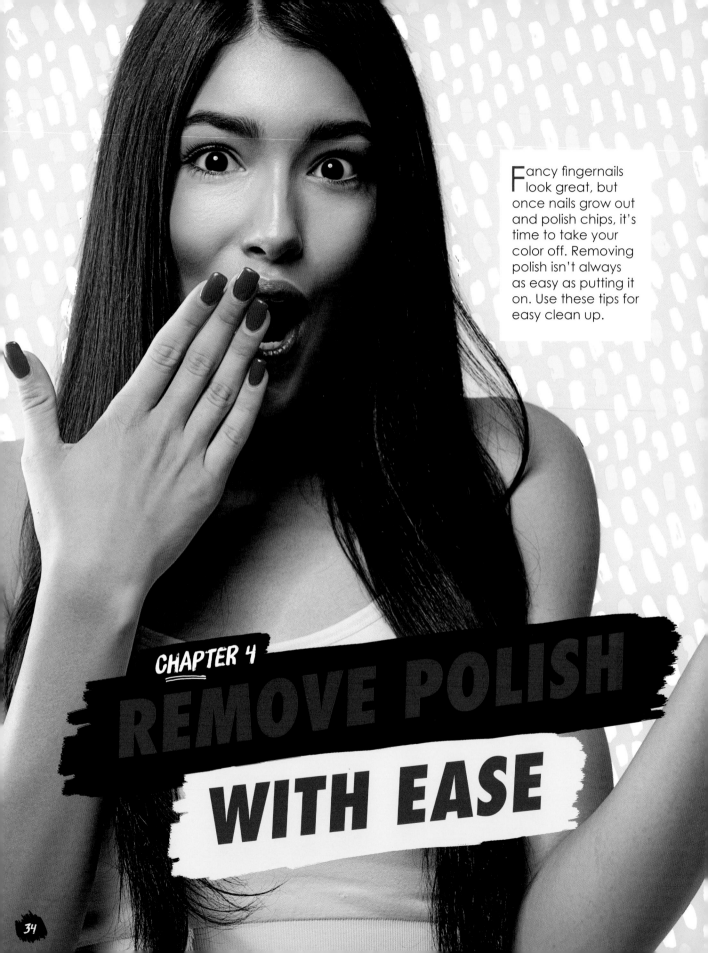

Fancy fingernails look great, but once nails grow out and polish chips, it's time to take your color off. Removing polish isn't always as easy as putting it on. Use these tips for easy clean up.

CHAPTER 4

REMOVE POLISH
WITH EASE

ACETONE OR NON-ACETONE REMOVER?

There are two types of nail polish remover: acetone and non-acetone. Learn about each to know which of these is best for you.

ACETONE POLISH REMOVERS

Acetone is a powerful chemical that's great at removing polish. But it is very harsh on skin. Your hands can stand up to acetone if it's only used once in a while. These types of removers are best for very dark polish colors, salon-style gel manicures, or for people who don't use polish often.

NON-ACETONE POLISH REMOVERS

Non-acetone removers use gentler chemicals than acetone. These chemicals don't remove polish as well as acetone. You'll need to do more scrubbing to remove stubborn polish. These products are best for removing light polish, for use with dry or sensitive skin and nails, and for those who use polish often.

SAFETY FIRST

Use caution when handling polish removers. The chemicals in them are flammable, so keep them away from heat sources. Even the fumes from nail polish remover are dangerous. They can create a vapor cloud. The cloud can create a flash fire when brought into contact with even a small candle flame.

SAVING SLOPPY PAINTERS

If you're one of those people who gets more polish on your skin than on your nails, try this simple trick.

WHAT YOU NEED:

white liquid glue

small, inexpensive paintbrush

+

base coat   +   nail color   +   top coat

WHAT YOU DO:

Step 1: Start with clean, shaped nails. Use the paintbrush to paint around your nails with glue. Get as close to sides of the nail as you can. Let glue dry completely.

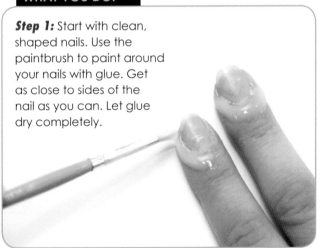

Step 2: Apply base coat.

Step 3: When base coat is dry to the touch, add a thin coat of nail color. Wait two to three minutes before applying a second coat. Once your second coat is dry, add a top coat.

Step 5: When your polish is dry, peel the glue off skin. Excess polish will peel off with the glue, leaving your nails neat and tidy.

SIMPLIFY POLISH CLEAN UP

Before your next at-home manicure, apply a little petroleum jelly to the skin around each nail with a cotton swab. Avoid getting petroleum jelly on the nail itself, because it will keep your polish from sticking. Once the petroleum jelly is applied, polish your nails as you normally would. Once nails are dry, wipe away petroleum jelly and, with it, any stray polish.

FLOSS AWAY STICKER WRAPS

Nail sticker wraps can add pizzazz to your nails, but they can be a real pain to remove. Next time you're ready to change wraps, soak your fingertips in warm water for five to 10 minutes. Then use a floss pick (yes, the same kind you use on your teeth) and wiggle it under the edge of the sticker wrap. Move the floss back and forth in a saw-like motion to gently pull the sticker off your nail.

REMOVE GLITTER POLISH

Yes, it's sparkly and eye-catching, but glitter polish can also be a pain to remove. Luckily, there is a trick that can help you. Tear five cotton balls in half, and soak them in polish remover. Then place one piece of cotton on each of your nails, and wrap them up with a piece of tin foil. The foil will keep the remover from evaporating and help it soak in to your polish. After about five minutes, pull off the foil and cotton. The glitter should be mostly gone.

RUBBING ALCOHOL

Can't find your nail polish remover? You might have something else that could do the trick. Any products with rubbing alcohol in them can remove polish. They'll just take a little more time to work. Spray or apply rubbing alcohol, hand sanitizer, hairspray, or perfume. Let the product sit for two minutes, then start scrubbing with a cotton ball or felt pad.

Remove with Felt

Next time you need to remove nail polish, try a felt square instead of a cotton ball. The texture of the felt will help scrub away stubborn polish. Buy white or light-colored felt, as it has fewer dyes. Cut it into 2-inch squares. Soak a square with remover and use it to wipe color off your nails.

USE MORE POLISH TO REMOVE POLISH

Another trick to remove polish without remover is to use more polish! Grab a bottle of nail polish or top coat. Apply it to your painted fingernails, then immediately wipe it off with a felt square. The fresh coat should pull off your old polish with it.

DON'T PEEL POLISH

You're sitting in study hall, and you're bored. But whatever you do, don't peel off your nail polish. Whether you're wearing traditional or gel polish, peeling it off can be harmful. If you start scraping or pulling at the old polish, you may end up damaging the top layer of your nail bed. This can seriously weaken your nails.

TAKE A BREAK FROM POLISH

If you wear nail polish daily, it can dry your nails. This makes them break more easily. Nail polish also keeps oxygen from your nails and the skin beneath them. That makes it more difficult to fight nail infections. Take time off from polish every now and then. Let your nails breathe to improve their overall health.

GET POLISH OFF YOUR SKIN

It's not uncommon to get a little nail polish on your skin when you're painting your nails. There are a few ways you can remedy that situation. Try these tips:

1. Let the nail polish dry. Trying to remove wet polish from your skin makes an even bigger mess.

2. Your own nails can be used as a tool. Use your nail to scratch off as much of the dry polish from the skin as you can. (Nail polish is not formulated to stick to skin the way it does nails.)

3. Use a cotton swab soaked in polish remover to clean up skin next to the nail.

DIY Polish ▶ ▶ ▶ ▶ ▶ Remover Jar

When you're in a hurry "dip and twist" nail polish remover jars are really handy. These jars contain both liquid polish remover and a sponge for scrubbing the polish off. You can buy one or make one yourself.

WHAT YOU NEED:

4-ounce glass jar with a lid   new kitchen sponge   scissors   nail polish remover

WHAT YOU DO:

Cut the sponge in half lengthwise. Tightly roll one piece of sponge, then wrap the other piece of sponge around the first. Put the tightly rolled sponges into the jar. Pour enough nail polish remover in the jar to soak the sponges.

HOW TO USE:

Put one finger at a time into the center of the rolled sponges. Twist your finger until all the polish is gone. Between uses, keep the cap tightly on the jar.

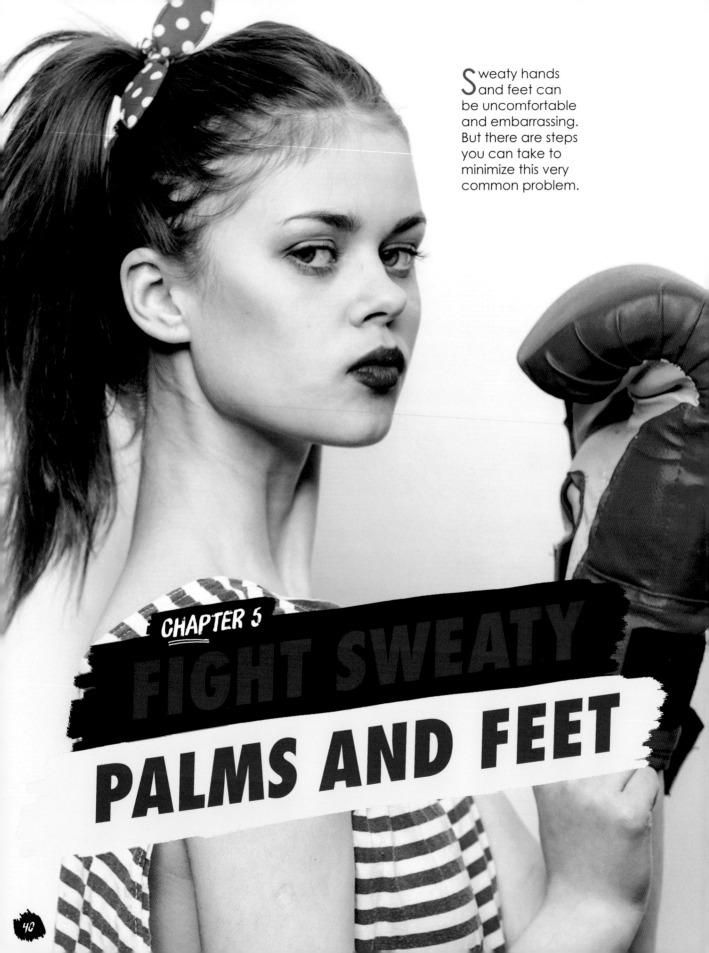

Sweaty hands and feet can be uncomfortable and embarrassing. But there are steps you can take to minimize this very common problem.

CHAPTER 5

FIGHT SWEATY PALMS AND FEET

ANTIPERSPIRANT

The same kind of antiperspirant you use on your underarms is also the first line of treatment for sweaty hands and feet. Antiperspirants are applied to the skin's surface, where sweat absorbs it. It essentially plugs your sweat ducts. When your body senses that the sweat ducts are plugged, it stops the flow.

Antiperspirants are available over-the-counter or by prescription from your doctor. The most widely used active ingredients in antiperspirants are metallic salts. Many antiperspirant manufacturers sell both regular and clinical-strength antiperspirants. Clinical-strength antiperspirants have more metallic salts. They're also more expensive.

HELPFUL TIPS

Tip#1 Start with regular–strength products. Only move on to stronger products if necessary.

Tip#2 With feet and hands, it's often most effective to apply product in the morning and again before bed.

Tip#3 Apply antiperspirant to dry skin. It lasts longer that way.

Let Feet
BREATHE

Wear sandals or shoes with mesh inserts to let your feet breathe. For dressier footwear, choose all-leather shoes without a lining or shoes lined with leather. Avoid shoes with plastic linings. They don't allow sweat to evaporate and don't absorb it. If your foot stays wet, there's a good chance bacteria will start growing.

ROTATE FOOTWEAR

If you have sweaty or even smelly feet, try not to wear the same pair of shoes two days in a row. Sweat is absorbed inside your shoes. They don't always dry out overnight. Damp shoes are the perfect breeding ground for bacteria and fungi. These icky little organisms can lead to bad smells and infections.

HOW MUCH SWEAT IS TOO MUCH?

Sweating is necessary to control body temperature. It cools your body when you need it. But some people sweat beyond what their bodies need to keep cool. The medical term for excessive sweating is *hyperhidrosis*. It's a fairly common problem that usually affects the palms, feet, and underarms.

It is normal to sweat when you're nervous or when it's hot out. But soaking through your shirt or socks every day is not normal. There are a number of medications or procedures that have been very successful in minimizing sweating. Talk to your family about getting medical attention if your problem persists.

BLACK TEA SOAK

If you're dealing with sweaty feet or hands, a tea soak may help solve your problem. The tannic acid in black tea kills bacteria and closes pores to reduce sweating. Boil two black tea bags in 2 cups of water. Remove the bags and add 2 quarts of cold water. Let the mixture cool, then soak your feet or hands for 30 minutes. Repeat daily until the sweating is under control.

GET SALTY

Sweaty feet themselves don't smell, but they can become a breeding ground for bacteria. Bacteria makes an acid byproduct that stinks. To stamp out the stink, treat yourself to a salt footbath. Dissolve one or two handfuls of kosher salt in a large tub of warm water. Soak your feet in this saltwater mixture for 20 minutes every day for two weeks. The salt will take moisture out of your skin, reducing the amount of bacteria that can survive there.

Watch What YOU EAT

Believe it or not, what you eat can affect how much you sweat. If you have super sweaty palms and feet, you should avoid caffeine and spicy foods. These types of foods raise your body temperature and your heart rate. This causes your sweat glands to go into overdrive.

TOSS YOUR NYLON SOCKS

Changing your socks can help you manage sweaty feet. Get rid of your nylon socks and replace them with socks that are at least 60-percent wool combined with nylon, polyester, or another man-made fiber. Socks that are 100-percent wool or cotton are not as good because they can't hold as much moisture without getting soggy.

SPRAY YOUR SHOES

Sweaty feet can cause smelly shoes, especially athletic shoes. You can use a disinfectant spray to revive your sneakers. Spray the inside of your shoe with the disinfectant. Then spray clean socks, put them in your shoes, and leave them overnight. The socks will make even more disinfectant soak into your shoes.

DRINK WATER

It may sound strange, but drinking more water can actually make you sweat less. Drinking fluids, especially water, can help lower your core temperature. A lower core temperature means less sweating.

CHAPTER 6
HEAL DRY HANDS AND FEET

Dry hands and feet may be the opposite of sweaty ones, but if they're too dry, they can be equally uncomfortable. Luckily there are ways to prevent and treat dry, itchy, and cracked hands and feet.

WASH SMARTER

Regular hand washing is necessary, but it can dry out your skin. To protect your hands, choose a mild soap, use lukewarm water, dry your hands, and apply a moisturizer right away. Some doctors suggest scrubbing just your palms when washing if your hands are particularly dry.

HEAL CRACKED HEELS

Dry, cracked heels are ugly and uncomfortable. Make them soft again using ingredients you probably have on hand — honey, milk, and orange juice. Honey seals in moisture. The vitamin A in milk nourishes skin. Orange juice has Vitamin C to aid with collagen production and give skin elasticity.

CHOOSE THE RIGHT MOISTURIZER

When it comes to moisturizing skin, there are two types of ingredients that do the most work. They are emollients and humectants. You can find the ingredients in lotions and moisturizers listed on the packages.

Emollients smooth your skin's surface by filling gaps between cells and helping the dead skin cells that are left behind stick together. Look for emollients such as lanolin, jojoba oil, isopropyl palmitate, propylene glycol linoleate, squalene, and glycerol stearate.

Humectants draw moisture from the environment, increasing the skin's water content. Look for humectants such as glycerin, hyaluronic acid, sorbitol, propylene glycerol, urea, and lactic acid.

DIY Moisturizer

Revive dry, cracked heels with this sweet homemade moisturizer.

WHAT YOU NEED:

1 cup of honey, slightly warmed

a spoonful of whole milk, slightly warmed

juice of one orange

pumice stone

 + + +

WHAT TO DO:

Step 1 Warm the honey slightly.

Step 2 Stir in milk and orange juice.

Step 3 Use pumice stone to rub off some of the callused skin.

Step 4 Spread a layer of the honey mixture onto your heels, massaging as you go.

Step 5 Put on a thick pair of socks and leave the mixture on at least 45 minutes. (You can leave it on overnight if you prefer.)

Step 6 Rinse with warm water and dry thoroughly.

READ MORE

Berne, Emma Carlson. *Nail Care Tips & Tricks.* Style Secrets. Minneapolis: Lerner Publications, 2016.

Meinking, Mary. *Creative Nail Art for the Crafty Fashionista.* Mankato, Minn.: Capstone Press, 2012.

Shoket, Ann, and Joanna Saltz. Seventeen *Ultimate Guide to Beauty: The Best Hair, Skin, Nails & Makeup Ideas for You.* Philadelphia: Running Press, 2012.

ABOUT THE AUTHOR

Mary Boone has written 34 nonfiction books for young readers on topics ranging from boy bands and fashion designers to crafts and cooking. She has also written for magazines including *Entertainment Weekly* and *People.* Mary and her family live in Tacoma, Washington, where the rain makes her hair forever frizzy.